Susan Hawthorne is a poet, publisher and academic. Her book, *Earth s Breath*, was shortlisted for the 2010 Judith Wright Poetry Award. She is Adjunct Professor in the Writing Program at James Cook University and the author of books of poetry, fiction and non-fiction, including co-editing (with Bronwyn Winter) the classic anthology, *September 11, 2001: Feminist perspectives*. Her latest collection of poetry is *Cow*.

VALENCE
CONSIDERING WAR THROUGH POETRY AND THEORY

Susan Hawthorne

SPINIFEX PRESS

for Renate

I wrote this poem in 2009 over several weeks. I had been thinking about war, about the roles played by my mother and grandmother in the twentieth-century wars. Then there was my mother's brother, imprisoned in Changi who never really recovered. How do you measure this loss?

1.

all day long the gods have been screaming
their prevalent song of war and pre-emptive strike
war leaves you gobsmacked words slaughtered in the throat

When we speak of fundamentalism, it's abstract. But such ideas have real effects on real people's lives. I had been thinking about language and about the many ways we talk about war. Think of rape. For how many centuries it has been used as a weapon of war. Every woman knew that. But only in the 1990s, after the mass rapes in a European country, did the wording of UN documents change.

Militarism, fundamentalism and the sex industry share the same ideology. Traumatised and vulnerable individuals become fodder for war and religion and pornography and prostitution (Hawthorne 2006a).

2.

that widowed ground has been filled with half-grown trees
almost impassable they are topped by yellow-crowned florets
along each side run sorrow pegs a means to navigate grief
against the fox-pelt cloud a woman stumbles tear-blinded
and half-demented her mind dismantling itself in a meltdown
so profound that buried poetry rises unbidden

the tiger's tongue is red at the root like a meridian
dissecting the fearful symmetry of its body
melting in the delicious buttery light of late afternoon
you dream of Petra's rock red caves imagine the bone dry
severed joints slumped like a ragdoll lumpy and disjoined
cranes settling above that old city in their precarious nests

no ladder long enough to reach them no florin
of pure gold to take you across that stream of air
you know you'd have to pay a bigger price for death
to mint that coinage sometimes you wish you'd learnt more
than just the Hebrew alphabet like raindrops in an eyelash
preciousness is nothingness against silk and stars

in your heart is a great hollow of pain like the chiselled
sound of a cello washing away the world's grief
a pilgrim on that Spanish trek to Santiago
your world turns illegible with its multiplying echoes
all you can do is eclipse the scream stuck in your throat
like a sow at sacrifice roped to interminable silence

The phrase 'that widowed ground' represents the bodies of women, of earth and of the loss of lives women have sustained – they have become a part of the great sense of loss that we experience in war. How do we 'navigate grief'? How navigate men's sense of entitlement over women's bodies. I know that feeling. My 20-year-old self, looking into possessive eyes. We are not lovers. But he has that look of a lust for conquest. A tremble of rape.

Places are infused with histories of violence. Years later, you can feel it. I was thinking of the remnants of the Spanish Civil War and the paths pilgrims tread. The echoes of war and the different ways it is carried out. We recognise the squeal of a slaughtered sow, it is not very different from a human scream.

3.

you study the index find grief sitting alongside greed
how dictionaries can turn destiny on a few letters
consider the difference between a water sprinkler
its afternoon sun of rainbows and laughter running
and a gas sprinkler its grey days of mud rag and bone
what a difference our meanings make of the world

you pick foxglove from the garden hoping for cure
there in the corner among the electric ferns is an old nude
green with moss her eyes crossed her forearms
broken at the wrist like a museum Venus her breath salty
you long for the nostalgia of flames foggy windowpanes
streets that cobble between old stone buildings

leaping shadows of gaslight in real-world film noir
galoshes keeping out the damp as you stroll the stream's
bank your lungs filled with the effigy of cold air
your destination was the Sistine Chapel but Rome on a
Monday has no secrets to give up to naïve backpackers
with budget time and so you wait twenty years

to see that composition now engraved in your dreams
arriving in Cairo might never have happened had you
travelled a day later not the shock of machineguns in the street
but in the hijacked plane sour breath a blurred video death
you talk the half dead tree fern back to life gentle it out
when the time comes to write the word grief yet again

In a poem you don't always know how a metaphor emerges, and suddenly I am confronted by the difference between water and gas. It shocks me, how such a simple thing can shift meaning. I am reminded how greed is connected to grief, through exploitation, by the desire to amass material goods at the expense of other people's lives.

The broken wrist of a Venus is considered a work of art. Mutilation elevated as nostalgia. The good old days of raw violence. But post-modern violence replicates what has always happened to women. You can never know quite who the enemy is. Is it the stranger, or more likely someone known to you? And how close we come to death sometimes. That hijacked flight I missed by travelling 24 hours earlier.

4.

on the tv last night the dead of Rwanda remain
where they died in the school buildings their bodies
preserved displayed as if part of an art installation
hands grasping at air mouths gasping a vacuum
skulls and leg bones sorted by size like hats cloths and rags
skins slung from a fork is it ever enough you never know

in advance what life-dice you have thrown the one where
you get to decide between flat buttons or round ones
on your jacket where foxes minks and seals sacrifice
their lives for your pleasure will you be the one whose foliage
screens the pool's liquid arabesque where cigarette smoke
wafts lazily in summer air not likely these chances are few

We sit in front of the TV, and it is no escape. As wars are rewound, as histories are written
and rewritten they are played out before our eyes. I am struck by the part played by luck,
because the other side of TV is glamour and celebrity. Rwanda is a nightmare, the horror
almost too hard to bear. In 2002, at another Women's World Congress in Uganda, the
driver whom three of us travelled with over a week, stopped the car one day and pointed
to a small river flowing between green fields. He told of how this river had been filled with
bodies.

In that same country, I learn about the torture of lesbians. It's like a blind being raised. The
light is too stark. How had I not seen this before? It takes me on a journey which I can
never abandon. Every year, I update the horrors. The war against lesbians as corrective rape
and torture (Hawthorne 2006b; 2011a).

5.

at the beginning of every year we ask whether
the killing spree is over for now all the soldiers
who heard earth's tinnitus ringing on the frontline
fly home walk through the front gate
cannot explain what they have seen have heard
that there is no longer any grace in the world

in the houses where women keep time with days
over stoves where hunger is the taste of childhood
and thirst a close neighbour no one dares to speak
peace is a mirage a vision at the edge of thought
cities stagnate and are separated from the people
countries are divided like pieces of cake

few speak against revenge slit the veins open
let the blood run a long-fingered violinist
plays a spree of notes emergent gravity looping
as a new virus explodes crossing all the man-made
boundaries taking off on its very own killing spree
rampaging through the gutters into the glare of air

My grandmother worked as nurse on a Red Cross ship in World War One. I was thinking of all that she had seen, of the hopelessness of war wounds, of the hunger of children, and of the waiting. And then the discovery of what had happened in the trenches, the effect of mustard gas. Not only were the lines drawn in Europe, in that same period the precursor lines of the Middle Eastern Wars were drawn. A country is not a cake to be divided.

6.

in Sabra and Shatila only bodies are left
shadows of screams echoes of eyes
that have stopped seeing stopped recording
a nation's memory will not unwrap when the chain
is nothing but missing links one by one
each memory becomes a wilderness

history is the mind of the patient
crumpled in the hallway after electric shock
fate is an uncut life sentence that fine stalk
of a body bent under the burden of guilt
a left handed idiom that itches beneath the skin
among the cedars of Lebanon gods once lived

This poem came from seeing the film, *Waltz with Bashir*, an animated film made by Ari Folman in search of memories he had lost following the 1982 Lebanon War. Like the patient referred to in the poem, the minds of those who participate as soldiers in war sometimes stop recording (Folman 2008).

Can we speak of abuse? Of the child whose memories flash back into her mind fifty years later. Searching for lost memories, steering around the boulders of fear blocking sight, running from recall (Stark 2011).

7.

you are writing hope in dust composing in a rapture
of fingertips by late afternoon ink stains make blotches
on your skin more patterns to unweave in memory of Penelope
your yarn unravelling night by night delaying that jury
of suitors choking on impatience the siren's voice sounds
it's you bound to the mast wanting to unmake those knots

the halflife of patience is short and betrayal follows in its wake
the hero sputters about the massacre the one he says
he didn't want his lips framing the victor's tale his face
telling another hands in pockets it's an ambivalent stance as if ash
and chaos and harrowing cries were not stalking his memory
whether justice is ever done or undone is a matter of want and will

Hope is an enduring element in war: hope that one day the war will end; hope that one's
family members and friends will return alive and safe. Can we question the hero, the one
who wears the medals, who can't bear to tell what really happened. And how war is
framed when it is finished depends on who gets to write the history.

Betrayal and treachery in the deepest wells of Dante's hell (Allighieri 2006: xv-xvi). There
can be no patience for those who betray their nearest and dearest, nor for turncoats who
thrive on chaos. How can we resist 'the legitimation of irresponsibility' (Kappeler 1995: 83).
The irresponsibility of patriarchal militaries. The institutionalisation of greed.

8.

revolutions have a tendency to unwind become slippery
as a greasy pole of jittery climbers how to disentangle
the fissures of power those times when absolutes are abstracted
followed by a contagion of swelling theories based on nothing
but a dream of marble palaces endless cases of whiskey temples
and statues to the self an insect grown large thorax like a shingled roof

behind stand the glassy-eyed disciples trilling with praise
promising to sacrifice all retreat to the woods
for fourteen years eat rotting peaches if need be
post-revolution days turn heavy all the dreams bludgeoned
knives appear and serrated philosophies become the latest thing
the way to leave your very own mark

Violence and corruption can become masters of even the most visionary struggles.
Victory is a powerful drug and you see it repeated: a good idea turns into a dictatorship.
Comradeship and unity are easy in the face of an enemy. Later, the rifts appear, ambition
overtakes justice.

9.

undoing hatred is a pilgrimage of hurt
power unwinds as much charge as a tangle of wire
we squirm in death's footprint caught in private fogs of affliction
all that energy ebbing in acts of fury the dying swan stilled exhausted
its wings wired its fluttering mind caged and broken
these many-mouthed furies iron-tongued grind their teeth all night long

uncurl your limbs stretch your spine
walk as if the sky's mantle is wrapped about your shoulders
when your breath evaporates look at the world with a split vision
imagine a hawk-eyed view of the oceans
from that height see the vast pastures of plankton
whalefood float with cuttlefish unoccupy your days

Not only people die in wars. Plants are burnt in raging fires; watercourses are polluted by chemicals; animals get caught in barbed wire or are stopped from migrating; or like the gorillas, their numbers further ravaged, their existence under severe threat. The idea of quiet, of having nothing to do, of having time to float on a calm sea seems impossible in the midst of war.

10.

you try to measure the valence of your feeling
runged like a ladder it is playing truant
these are the astonishments of life cunning as gravity's spectrum
this morning someone spoke of the desire to be unlimbed
this evening you race to the vet on a false alarm for the dog
how to measure that strength of bond is it like helium or xenon

at the time of vespers a huge flock of lorikeets
sweeps along the street a wave with thousands
of particles like a symphony filled with quavers
bones splinter in earth's chemicals accrue new geographies
anchor on thin strings of narrative built syllable
by syllable valences as permeable as love

During war, life continues. Whether it's the emergencies of pets or children, or the mad rushings of a flock of noisy birds. And even love persists, indeed for some, it is heightened by the prospect of losing it so soon.

The amputee of war is fetishised by the practitioners of sado-masochism, who will play at torture in their well controlled dungeons. They cry, Stop, they cry, Rumsfeld. With contempt, appropriating pain (Hawthorne 2011b: 93-4).

11.

pharaohs haunt the tight tendon of night
it is dreaming that makes us human
footprints tracking their own unstoppable destiny
fighting homesickness you wing across the void the planet
hollowing on the verge of collapse while some human-made
god keeps on with his incessant dictation

is it the dead who keep you awake at night
a vision of a planet's suicide attempt
limbs severed life hung in balance
what kind of shaming will it take to unpurse the future
in the moments before the noose tightens a gutful
of interglacial moments to ruminate on the planet's past

a species whose collective search for jewels took the wrong
road in pursuit of furnaces and smelting of iron
instead of firelight and song the drying tips
of trees turned into barbs and missiles
overhead sky anvils crash and blast presaging the drop
of earth's floor faster than a game of drop the hanky

The history of war is long, too long. War is profitable and so 'unpursing the future' is highly unlikely while the profit motive drives economies and wars. But to continue is to put the planet at risk. The nuclear power plants will melt down, spreading an invisible poison. The smelters will resume but the children will not be around to play drop-the-hanky. I wonder how long the planet can hang out, why not just crash those thunderous clouds and let the earth slide away (Hawthorne 2011c).

12.

you dream of flight with wings with claw some days
you sob because all the elegies for the dead all the strings
played with furious pathos will not stop the clot of war

I do not finish with a sense of hope. Indeed, I feel a great sense of hopelessness about the future. War is glorified. The heroes keep dying. The men keep signing up; and the women join up too. The birds, the beautiful sea eagles that fly past the house, now that is freedom (Hawthorne 2009: 7).